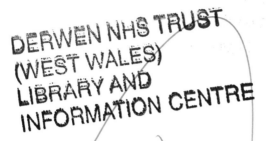
ON BEING A DOCTOR

Redefining medical professionalism for better patient care

REBECCA ROSEN AND STEVE

The King's Fund is an independent charitable foundation working for better health, especially in London. We carry out research, policy analysis and development activities, working on our own, in partnerships, and through grants. We are a major resource to people working in health, offering leadership and education courses; seminars and workshops; publications; information and library services; and conference and meeting facilities.

Published by:

King's Fund
11–13 Cavendish Square
London W1G 0AN
www.kingsfund.org.uk

© King's Fund 2004

Charity registration number: 207401

First published 2004

ISBN 1 85717 475 5

Available from:

King's Fund Publications
11–13 Cavendish Square
London W1G 0AN
Tel: 020 7307 2591
Fax: 020 7307 2801
Email: publications@kingsfund.org.uk
www.kingsfund.org.uk/publications

Edited by Alan Dingle
Typeset by Grasshopper Design Company
Cover design by Minuche Mazumdar
Printed and bound in Great Britain by Hobbs

Contents

About the authors

Rebecca Rosen
Fellow, Health Policy, King's Fund

Rebecca works half-time as a Fellow in Health Policy at the King's Fund and half-time as a GP in south-east London. Her current health policy interests include chronic disease management, new professional roles in primary care and access to specialist care. Her work on chronic disease management spans national policy analysis and the local organisation of chronic care services in primary care. Rebecca is a trustee of Asthma UK and Chair of a small charity promoting closer relationships between scientists and artists.

Steve Dewar
Director, Development, King's Fund

Steve specialises in political ideas for health care, professionalism and regulation, and the nature of personal and organisational learning. As a non-medic with a background in operational research, he has nine years' experience in the NHS as a researcher and public health specialist, and as a change manager in a district general hospital. He has written extensively on a range of health care issues.

Acknowledgements

Many people have helped to shape the ideas in this discussion paper.
Our thanks are due to the participants in the joint King's Fund, Leeds
Castle seminar on medical professionalism, held in March 2003, and to
those who attended one of the three seminars on this subject held at
the King's Fund during April and May 2004 (*see* Appendix: List of
seminar participants, pp 54–55). We are also very grateful to Nizam
Mamode and Cyril Chantler for their comments on earlier drafts, and to
Clare Bawden and Isabella Kpobie for their administrative support.
Particular thanks are due to Sir Donald Irvine for many helpful
discussions and suggestions during the course of this work.

Summary

This is a critical time for the future of the medical profession, with unprecedented challenges arising from the changing expectations of patients, government and managers. Doctors remain 'professionals' but the traditional image of what this means in practice – a selfless clinician, motivated by a strong ethos of service, equipped with unique skills and knowledge, in control of their work and practising all hours to restore full health to 'his' or 'her' patients – is increasingly outdated.

While individual doctors remain highly trusted, the profession as a whole needs to demonstrate better its overriding duty to serve patients' interests and to show that it can respond to changing public and political expectations. To sustain and build trust in the profession, doctors need to ensure that their practice reflects the behaviour expected of them.

Drawing on discussion and debate among a wide range of stakeholders, this paper examines recent challenges to the profession, explores how a new compact between key stakeholders might be formed, and offers a way forward to redefining medical professionalism for the future. Above all, it is intended to encourage further debate on this vitally important issue.

Challenges to medical professionalism

The first duty of a doctor must be to ensure the well being of patients and to protect them from harm – this responsibility lies at the heart of medical professionalism. Patients expect doctors to be technically competent, open and honest, and to show them respect. By demonstrating these qualities, doctors earn the trust that makes their professional status and privileges possible.

Yet the freedom that doctors once enjoyed to define acceptable standards of care and to control the content and organisation of their work is under pressure on a number of fronts:

- Widely publicised incidents, such as the unauthorised retention of organs at Alder Hey Children's Hospital Trust and the unacceptable practice of paediatric heart surgeons in Bristol, have revealed failures by the profession to stay in tune with prevailing public values and maintain standards.

- There is an increasing expectation among the general public for timely and convenient access to an ever-wider range of services, provided with greater openness and accountability.

- There is a growing demand among patients for more responsive consultations with doctors that will enable them to participate in clinical decision-making.

- There is increased managerial control over medical work as well as perceived medical resistance to this and to wider government reform of the health service.

- New ways of working have developed, including more team and multi-disciplinary working and an increasing diversification of medical roles to include academic, managerial, strategic and advisory functions.

- Changes in doctors' working conditions have taken place, driven partly by European legislation restricting working hours and by a higher proportion of doctors, mainly women, combining work with childcare responsibilities.

A changing compact

An implicit 'compact' between doctors, patients and government has underpinned the working of the National Health Service (NHS) since its inception in 1948. With the formation of the NHS, the government guaranteed universal access to health care. A self-regulating medical profession was expected to maintain clinical standards and work with strictly limited resources in return for significant clinical freedom and minimal accountability. And the public accepted its health care rights from government with associated tax obligations to fund an NHS free at the point of delivery.

But, as outlined above, the original partners in the compact are changing their expectations. In addition, new stakeholders, such as NHS managers, new government departments and European regulatory bodies – each with a legitimate interest in health services and each pursuing a wide range of interests – want to have a say in the compact. The perception that doctors have not responded adequately to the expectations of these groups, nor to the expectations of patients, lies behind many of the criticisms currently levelled at them.

In practice, these shifts have already triggered many changes within the profession. The General Medical Council (GMC) updated the standards it expects of doctors in its publication *Good Medical Practice* (General Medical Council 2001). More lay people are now involved in the GMC and the medical Royal Colleges. Medical school and postgraduate curricula are incorporating the teaching of professionalism, and many individual doctors are developing innovative ways to support patients as active partners in making clinical decisions.

Yet many dilemmas and challenges remain. A modern definition of medical professionalism is needed that equips doctors to deal with them in ways that reflect prevailing social and political values and that are clearly understood by the public.

Responding to the challenges in practice

A series of case studies is used to illustrate the dilemmas raised by recent challenges, and explore how a new notion of medical professionalism might help:

■ **New out-of-hours arrangements** With the new GP contract in 2004 came the end of GPs' duty to provide out-of-hours (OOH) cover. Up to 90 per cent of GPs are expected to pull out of providing OOH care. The notion of modern medical professionalism argued in this paper requires open dialogue between doctors, patients and other stakeholders to negotiate the roles and responsibilities of all parties – particularly doctors. But patient groups were not directly involved in the development of OOH policy, and a recent poll indicates that about one-third of patients are unhappy with the arrangements. GPs face a major professional challenge in ensuring that the quality of OOH services – now commissioned by primary care trusts (PCTs) – is sufficiently high to warrant handing over clinical responsibility of their registered patients each night. Whatever new challenges present themselves, disengagement and a willingness to let others take responsibility for the quality of patient care are not options. Active participation in developing new and better services must become the norm. Just as importantly, PCTs should be willing to acknowledge problems and allocate the resources needed to solve them.

■ **Waiting list initiatives** Government and NHS managers have responded to public demand for faster treatment with initiatives such as centralised booking systems and revising the balance between new patients, follow-up patients and urgent patients in outpatient clinics. But this focus on faster access to care for all patients may prevent doctors from achieving the best clinical outcomes for some individuals. Structural changes in the NHS have reduced the role of doctors in hospital management and marginalised them in the reorganisation of services. A new compact might explicitly require doctors to help their organisation improve services. But it should also include a reciprocal obligation on the part of policy-makers and managers to involve doctors more directly in the development of health services and to create an environment in which best practice can thrive.

■ **Clinical judgement and individual entitlement to care**
A long-standing dilemma for doctors has been how to respond to patient requests for additional tests and investigations when the doctor's own clinical judgement is that such tests are not clinically necessary. The management of headache in primary care illustrates this dilemma. Brain tumours account for less than 0.1 per cent of headaches, but many patients who visit their GP with persistent headaches will be worried about this as a possible cause and request a brain scan to assess this possibility. Medical professionalism requires open, honest and respectful consultations between doctors and patients in which constraints on expectation and differences of opinion are acknowledged and discussed. Recent US research emphasises the shared responsibility of doctors, patients and health care providers to place patient interest at the centre of decisions about health care – but not to the exclusion of all other factors. It stresses the obligation of health insurers, as well as doctors, to be open about the limits to available services, arguing that this is particularly important for the professional integrity of individual doctors.

■ **Changes to professional regulation and accountability** Government and the doctors' regulatory body (GMC) have both responded to pressures for greater accountability of the medical profession with a number of major initiatives. These include: the new consultant contract, with its increased job planning and managerial control over the content of medical work; formal appraisal systems; and proposals for appraisal-based revalidation that, from 2005, will require doctors to demonstrate to the GMC their continuing competence in return for a licence to practise. But how do these initiatives by state and profession interact? Will they be sufficient to assure the public, and patients in particular, of doctors' technical skills and knowledge? And what impact are these initiatives having on the profession? An increasingly complex system for ensuring accountability can undermine the professionalism it is supposed to safeguard. Doctors may feel less inclined to behave altruistically if they are excessively scrutinised. The profession may need to open a debate about the combined impact of these changes and what other reforms may be necessary.

The way forward

It is clear that we need to find new ways of ensuring a healthy and self-confident medical profession for the future. Once in place, this will help to build the trust we regard as essential to ensuring that the compact between doctors and other stakeholders will sustain the medical profession in future.

But how will this modern form of medical professionalism be defined and put into practice? The paper makes some specific suggestions:

■ **Put patient interests at the heart of professional practice**
A renewed emphasis on ensuring professional standards and behaviours are centred on patient interests. Acknowledging that patients pursue multiple interests that may be inconsistent or in tension with each other, doctors must find new ways to link professional standards to explicit debate about the dilemmas of modern practice.

■ **Define a new compact** The 'compact' between doctors, government and the public must be redefined to include other, newer partners, such as NHS managers and diverse patient groups. Where the expectations of different partners conflict, there should be frank and free discussion. The compact must embrace a new level of responsiveness to patient interests and a focus on identifying professional standards that are in tune with prevailing values and expectations.

The compact must also reflect a duty among doctors to engage in improving health services with a reciprocal obligation on the part of government and managers to develop and implement health policy that allows the highest standards of professional practice to flourish. These changes should help to rebuild public trust in doctors, which has been eroded by the current climate of criticism. The changes would include: active patient and public involvement in the work of medical institutions; enhanced roles for doctors in the development and implementation of health policy; high-quality debate about the dilemmas of professional practice in the media; and national and local consultations between doctors and patients on planned service changes.

■ **Strengthen medical leadership** The medical establishment – in the shape of the Royal Colleges, the GMC, the medical schools and other institutions – should take the lead in translating the terms of this new compact into everyday practice. They must create an environment where 'acting professionally' is seen to embrace the achievement of the highest clinical standards, respect for the interests of individual patients and engagement with the development and improvement of health services.

■ **Define doctor/manager roles clearly** The relationship between NHS managers and doctors must be clarified in order to establish who is best qualified to do what in the quest to improve health services. Structural change is needed in the organisation of health care management in order to re-engage doctors in the improvement of health services, and to develop better working relationships and more closely aligned objectives between clinical and non-clinical managers.

Introduction

The King's Fund is an independent organisation committed to improving the quality of health and health care. We see the involvement of doctors as central to improving care. Whether it is a case of renewing their relationship with patients or helping to reform the health care system as a whole, doctors need to be confident in their roles, clear about their responsibilities, committed to doing the best for patients and fully engaged in the institutions and political processes that are bringing about service improvement.

We believe that individual patients, health care organisations and government need to work collaboratively with doctors to improve health services and to ensure that the patient's interests lie at the heart of all medical practice. This requires a definition of professionalism that is directly relevant to the day-to-day work of doctors. Building on a series of seminars that we have held on this subject, the King's Fund hopes to stimulate wider debate about 'modern professionalism'. The debate should aim to create a definition of professionalism that is shared by doctor, patient, policy-maker, manager and government minister alike. This new professionalism should inspire trust in everyone who has dealings with doctors and make possible the full engagement of doctors in improving health care.

How change is affecting doctors

We all rely on doctors to treat and advise us. We see them as central to modern health care services. We expect them to act in our own best interests in individual consultations and to pursue society's collective interests by providing high-quality services. Our faith that doctors will fulfil these responsibilities is based on our trust in them as professionals who are motivated by an ethos of public service, work to high ethical standards, possess excellent technical skills and knowledge and have effective arrangements for self-regulation. These are, after all, the basic characteristics of any profession.

Yet the medical profession is currently experiencing unprecedented challenges. Patients and the Government alike are raising their expectations of how doctors, and the health services in which they work, should perform. In this, patients and the Government have been influenced by many factors including:

- widely publicised incidents that reveal failures of doctors to regulate themselves effectively and maintain standards
- a growing demand among patients for more convenient services and more responsive consultations with doctors that will enable them to participate in clinical decision-making
- an increasing expectation among the general public that all professions should demonstrate greater openness and accountability.

If the medical profession is to meet these expectations, it needs to be more actively engaged with patients (through patient groups) and with the wider public (many of whom will be patients in the future). Leaders of the profession will need to establish a culture that helps doctors meet the demands of well-informed patients. And the collective institutions of the profession must form a range of new relationships that will enable them to respond to society's expectations.

Similarly, the relationship between doctors and the organisations in which they work is changing. This is partly a leadership issue: how can doctors continue to exert a positive influence through a professionalism based on public interest, when many of their traditional freedoms are being eroded by the growth in managerial control? Although doctors are central to the provision of health care, their input to the development and implementation of health policy is often selective and does not necessarily represent the views of those doctors who will be affected by the change.

The nature of modern professionalism

We see modern professionalism as a dynamic concept, rooted in a long tradition of service and high ethical standards, and shaped by public expectations. At the heart of modern professionalism lies a duty to protect patient interests and enhance their experiences of health care. Linked to this lies a commitment to ensure that the clinical behaviour of individual doctors and the standards set by its collective institutions are consistent with current social values. However, organisational and political reforms, undertaken to improve patients' experiences of health care, may increasingly conflict with professional views about how best to serve patient interests, triggering tensions between doctors, managers and government.

In response, modern medical professionalism should actively promote engagement between doctors, patients, medical institutions, policy-makers and a variety of other stakeholders interested in improving health care. Doctors need to respond to the many conflicts of interest that arise in their individual practice and in relation to organisational and policy developments in ways that show their commitment to their patients, thus helping to build public trust. Using this applied view of medical professionalism to resolve these difficult issues would also improve the self-confidence of the medical profession and enable doctors to play a more effective role in the improvement of health care.

Our intentions

This paper is aimed at everyone who has an interest in defining modern medical professionalism, including doctors and leaders of the medical profession, government and the wider policy community, other health care professionals and managers, patients and the general public. We concede that focusing solely on doctors narrows the scope of the paper, but argue that this keeps the analysis within manageable bounds. We also believe that the decisions and practice styles of doctors remain of central importance in health care, accounting for the majority of expenditure and often determining the quality of patient experience.

We examine the many recent challenges to the medical profession and what they reveal about differences between the values and expectations of the profession, the general public and government. We discuss how new relationships might be formed between doctors, patients and other stakeholders. We show how medical professionalism might be constructively applied to a range of current challenges. And we look at how doctors and their professional organisations might strengthen public trust in the medical profession and work to ensure a continued focus on improving the patient experience in the future.

The social and political context of medical professionalism

Defining 'modern professionalism'

The first duty of a doctor must be to ensure the well being of patients and to protect them from harm – this responsibility lies at the heart of medical professionalism. Patients expect doctors to be technically competent, open and honest, and to show them respect. By demonstrating these qualities, doctors earn the trust that makes their professional status and privileges possible.

In the absence of a single, widely accepted definition of professionalism, we have drawn upon the work of Irvine (Irvine 2003) and others (Cruess R, Cruess S 2003; Medical Professionalism Project 2002) to suggest that the concept has four basic characteristics. These are:
- a calling or vocation linked to public service and altruistic behaviour
- the observance of explicit standards and ethical codes
- the ability to apply a body of specialist knowledge and skills
- a high degree of self-regulation over professional membership and the content and organisation of work.

These core characteristics of professionalism are as relevant today as they have ever been. Yet the way in which they are applied in practice must be regularly reviewed so that medical professionals can stay in tune with the prevailing expectations of society. The profession's perceived failure to respond to changes in these expectations lies behind many of the current criticisms levelled at doctors.

The traditional image of doctors is of selfless individuals prepared to 'go the extra mile' for their patients at all hours of the day or night. But the medical profession should ask itself how far this image remains relevant in today's conditions. European working-time directives are legally binding, clinical teamwork is replacing personal 24-hour responsibility, and expectations of a better work–life balance are reducing the willingness of doctors (and other health professionals) to work long hours.

Similarly, observing ethical codes is fundamental to what it means to be a doctor. But sometimes these codes create moral dilemmas: for example, the desire to respect the preferences of individual patients may conflict with the requirement to respond to the needs of the general population. And ethical imperatives may change over time: for example, the emphasis on respecting patient autonomy and patient choice has grown in recent years.

When it comes to knowledge and skills, similar challenges arise. Patients expect their doctors to be technically competent, seeing this as a central part of their professionalism. But rapid scientific advances make it increasingly difficult for doctors to keep abreast of new knowledge. Also, information technology is changing the way in which doctors practise. They may, for example, have immediate access to electronic information that can support their technical knowledge and help their decision-making. Patients themselves are better informed and more questioning in their attitudes. Doctors may therefore need to see themselves not just as the repository of expert knowledge but also as an interpreter, helping patients to understand the mass of available information.

Finally, there are difficulties over self-regulation. As well as controlling entrance into their profession, doctors won considerable control over the content and organisation of their work when the NHS was launched. However, widely publicised medical failures have led to major reforms in the way doctors regulate themselves. In addition, the Government's more centralised approach to running the NHS, based on setting specific performance targets, has led managers to take greater control over the organisation and content of work that was previously managed by individual doctors.

Since the foundation of the NHS, doctors have enjoyed considerable freedom over how they demonstrate the core characteristics of professionalism in their day-to-day practice. This has inevitably led to wide variations in the way doctors practise, and equally wide variations in the sensitivity they display toward patient preferences. Various formal mechanisms have emerged for challenging behaviour thought to be unacceptable. These have included complaint procedures, legal action by patients against their doctors and referral to the GMC.

However, these have not been the only challenges to the prevailing standards of professional practice. Many others have emerged, and these are summarised below.

Current challenges to medical professionalism

Extreme cases of professional failure

Widely publicised failures by doctors have cast doubt on the medical profession's ability to protect the interests of patients over and above its own interests: for example, in the cases of the Bristol paediatric heart surgeons (Mayor 2001) and the liver surgeon Steven Walker (Carter 2004). Similarly, the case of Alder Hey Children's Hospital Trust, where children's organs were retained for research purposes without the clear consent of relatives, showed the degree to which the profession was out of touch with public expectations of doctors' behaviour. Doctors are also accused of responding inadequately to public demand for timely and convenient access to care – as shown by the persistent 'waiting list' problems in the NHS. This has led to further charges that doctors are too willing to put their own interests (in private practice) above those of patients.

Changing public expectations

Social change has led to increased expectations of health care among the general public:

- The growth of consumerism means that people are less willing to tolerate waiting lists and badly organised services.
- Doctors are increasingly being held accountable for their performance.
- An increase in personal wealth for many people means that they can buy alternative therapies, second opinions and access to other health services.
- Public trust in all authority figures – including doctors – has declined.

Changes in the expectations of individual patients

Different patients will obviously have different expectations of how doctors should behave, and their expectations will vary depending on the kind of illness they are experiencing. Nevertheless, we can identify some general trends in what patients have come to expect:

- They are less tolerant of paternalistic styles of medical practice and expect to enjoy increasing respect for individual autonomy.
- Improved access to medical information has equipped patients to request specific interventions and to question proposed clinical plans.
- Patients are less deferential: they are more likely to challenge doctors and seek second opinions.
- Patients do not want to be told that their medical needs are less important than somebody else's. Although the NHS has limited resources, many are reluctant to accept that this should affect their 'right' to the treatment they want.

Changes in the Government's expectations of doctors

In its approach to reforming public services, particularly the NHS, the Government has shown a determination to end politically damaging media coverage, to improve value for money from public spending and to champion selected patient preferences, particularly timely access. This raises various challenges for doctors:

- growing expectations of accountability for productivity and performance
- cross-party agreement on the need to improve the patient experience of health services
- reviews of the regulation of doctors and other health care professionals
- new institutions to scrutinise the work of doctors and investigate complaints
- the requirement to balance the needs of individual patients against those of whole populations.

Increases in centralised managerial control over medical work

In recent years, the efficiency of the NHS has been one of the most widely debated issues during general election campaigns. It is not surprising therefore that politicians have put pressure on those who work in the health service – particularly doctors – to improve the delivery of health care. In so doing, Government has often sought to change the way in which services are managed.

But the recent emphasis on achieving national targets has meant that managers are seeking tighter control over the organisation and content of medical work. For example, making consultants employees of the hospital in which they work, and thus (theoretically) accountable to the chief executive, has given managers more opportunity to control the workloads of consultants and monitor their performance.

These changes affect the context for modern professionalism in various ways:

- Technological developments, such as centralised booking systems, have taken some direct control over patients and their care away from frontline doctors.
- Political pressure over waiting lists has forced changes in hospital organisation that may challenge clinical priorities and give managers some control over prioritising patients.
- The introduction of external targets has led to more formal rules and policies, more surveillance, and the use of incentives and sanctions that reduce professional autonomy (Harrison 2003).
- Differences between the priorities of managers and those of clinical staff have increased tensions between the two groups.
- Targeted and ring-fenced resources have made it harder to introduce clinician-led developments that are not in line with organisational priorities.
- The roles of allied health professionals have been developed, resulting in more multi-disciplinary teams for specialised care (for example, diabetes and stroke).
- Widespread use of information technology and clinical information systems has increased the data available for monitoring and auditing performance.

Changes in doctors' expectations of their own working conditions

After years of putting in long hours, many doctors now have their working day restricted by European legislation. This and other factors have led to new patterns of work. Some of the most important changes are:

- the reorganisation of doctors into teams rather than hierarchical 'firms', thus enabling cross-cover and the sharing of clinical responsibility for patients

- increased specialisation, which means that doctors now have highly technical expertise in narrower fields – thus making them more interdependent
- increasing diversification of medical roles to include academic, managerial, strategic/advisory and commercial functions
- the 'feminisation' of the medical workforce, with a higher proportion of female doctors combining work with childcare responsibilities
- doctors seeking a new work–life balance, and thus sometimes unable to participate fully in specialities or professional activities that are less accommodating.

The response to these challenges

Taken together, these challenges indicate the areas where members of the public, professionals, politicians, patients, policy-makers and journalists seem to differ in their views of what doctors should do and how they should behave. Many of the people and institutions that shape the roles of doctors have already started to respond to these challenges:

- There have been significant improvements in public involvement with the GMC and several Royal Colleges.
- Appraisal and revalidation are starting to affect the way doctors maintain their skills and knowledge and reflect upon their relationships with patients.
- The curricula of medical schools are paying more attention to professionalism.
- Many doctors are changing the way they consult with patients, using new techniques to enable them to share in clinical decision-making.

In response to these challenges – and in particular to the case of the Bristol paediatric heart surgeons – the GMC has updated the professional standards expected of doctors. Its publication *Good Medical Practice* (General Medical Council 2001) specifies the standards of practice expected when doctors deal with individual patients, when doctors deal with their colleagues and when doctors update their skills. Based on extensive consultation with patients, the publication embodies current expectations about respect for patients and their active involvement in clinical decisions and provides a framework for appraisal and revalidation.

Good Medical Practice is essentially an operational handbook for the medical profession. It is a practical response to the changed expectations of those who have a legitimate interest in the role of the modern doctor. This is welcome as far as it goes, but several questions remain:

- What can doctors do to ensure that modern professionalism is properly understood and effectively applied?
- How can doctors maintain their dialogue with external constituencies so that standards of good practice continue to satisfy prevailing social and political expectations?
- How can the profession continue to respond to the challenges listed above in a positive rather than defensive fashion?

We believe that a new definition of medical professionalism would offer a way of understanding these challenges and resolving them.

A suggested framework for debate

To enable modern medical professionalism to flourish, we suggest that doctors adopt a new approach. The leaders of the medical profession should:
- accept that a range of new stakeholders now has a legitimate interest in defining professionalism, and acknowledge that these stakeholders may be pursuing different interests

- recognise the importance to modern professionalism of strengthening trust in doctors
- develop the compact between doctors and other stakeholders, as an effective basis for renegotiating the standards and values expected of the medical profession
- ensure that the leaders of medical institutions help to translate these expected standards into everyday practice
- tell the public and other stakeholders what can be expected of doctors and what are the limits to their role
- raise public confidence in the ability of doctors to meet current expectations in their daily clinical practice, making possible a high trust approach to medical regulation and accountability.

Accepting new stakeholders

We have suggested that some of the challenges faced by doctors arise from conflicts of interest between clinicians, patients, government and others. Stakeholders with a legitimate interest in the role of doctors are an increasingly heterogeneous group (*see* Figure 1, p 24) with a diverse range of interests.

Within the profession itself there is enormous variety. Medical work ranges from high-technology, hospital-based specialities, such as neuro-surgery, to community-oriented branches of paediatrics and psychiatry. Doctors can be anything from full-time hospital consultants to part-time, single-handed GPs. They carry out an increasing variety of roles as clinicians, managers, academics, strategists and advisers.

With these diverse roles come multiple and at times conflicting interests. Doctors' clinical goal is to achieve the best clinical outcomes. But they also pursue job satisfaction and value the ability to control the content of their work. Some aim to maximise their income through private practice and other private work. Academics must combine clinical duties with the need to win research grants, publish papers and teach students. Medical managers, in particular, have to balance their clinical work with individual patients with the pursuit of better health care for whole populations.

The other groups of stakeholders have become equally diverse. When the NHS was founded, 'the public' could have been crudely divided into two groups: current NHS patients and future NHS patients. Now, the public has diversified into many categories, including individual patients, patient groups, consumers of 'wellness' services, lay representatives in Royal Colleges, and medical associations. These stakeholders also pursue a range of interests, including achieving the best possible clinical outcomes; ensuring that medical care is consistent with personal values and expectations; ensuring that patients enjoy autonomy in clinical consultations; and pursuing 'consumerist' aspirations, such as obtaining timely and convenient access to health services.

'Government' too has become more fragmented. The devolved assemblies in Wales and Scotland, the Cabinet Office and the European Parliament (to name but a few) all now have key roles alongside the Department of Health. Here too a variety of interests are being pursued. There are clear political objectives, such as improving the quality of public services in line with patient interests, minimising politically damaging media coverage of the NHS, and ensuring electoral success. Europe's interests include the harmonisation of policies across member states.

The evolution of managers as a distinct group is also important, given their key role of implementing government policy within the NHS. The interests of this group include: improving services in line with government targets; the strategic development of health services; job satisfaction and career progression.

Strengthening trust in doctors

Trust is a fragile commodity. It has to be built through repeated encounters, between doctors and patients and between government and the leaders of the medical profession. Trust can be partly rebuilt by improving the way in which encounters with patients – and with their carers and relatives – are conducted. Doctors could, for example, do more to build trust through honest, open and empathic communications (Burkitt Wright, Holcombe, Salmon 2004). Consultations of this kind would enhance confidence in doctors and the other members of the clinical team, and provide patients with the advice and information they need to allay their fears.

We also need to consider the impact that health care organisations have on trust in the overall system of care; in the UK this typically means the NHS, although the role of private providers is growing. If doctors yield to the temptation of blaming problems on 'the system' – over which they have no control – this will do little to renew trust. It is important for doctors to engage with the wider health care system, and in particular to get involved in efforts to improve it – although there are currently many barriers to this (*see* Dilemmas in professional practice, pp 28–46).

Thirdly, the onus is upon medical institutions to lead the process. This is starting to happen, as shown by the GMC's publication of *Good Medical Practice*. Royal Colleges, medical schools, postgraduate deans and others have an important role to play in encouraging doctors to get involved in organisational and service development as part of their professional role. Medical leaders also need to support the development of new styles of consultation, a more open exchange of information and greater accountability for performance and outcomes.

Developing a new compact between doctors and other stakeholders

The NHS was founded on a new relationship between government, the medical profession and the public, expressed through an implicit compact (Ham and Alberti 2002):

■ The government guaranteed universal access to care within the NHS budget.
■ The profession maintained clinical standards and delivered care to patients.
■ The public accepted its health care rights from the government, delivered to appropriate standards by the profession, and paid taxes to fund the NHS.

As part of this compact, the government continued to allow the medical profession considerable autonomy in return for government control over the NHS budget and national policy. It is widely perceived that there was a degree of collusion between government and profession, with doctors agreeing to work within the limits of government policy in return for the ability to decide on clinical priority within available funds (rationing) without interference from politicians.

Doctors have continued to enjoy this autonomy and freedom to self-regulate until relatively recently. However, we have shown that the stakeholders in the compact are becoming more numerous, and that the limited ability of patients and the wider public to influence health service developments and organisational change has become unacceptable.

We suggest that a new compact is needed, with more open engagement between the medical profession and other stakeholders. Patients, professionals, government and other parties will all have their own views about what modern professionalism should look like. Taking the patient's interests as the central focus of medical professionalism, the views of each stakeholder need to be fully explored in order to identify appropriate responses to the challenges facing the profession. As we have seen, these challenges include: ethical dilemmas; under-performing doctors or hospitals; policies and organisational developments that constrain the clinical judgements of doctors; conflicts of interest between stakeholders; and the failure to maintain skills and competence.

Figure 1 shows the stakeholders in the new compact and the role of the media and other information and communication technologies. The media play an increasingly important role by disseminating information

FIGURE 1: Stakeholders and relationships for a new medical professionalism

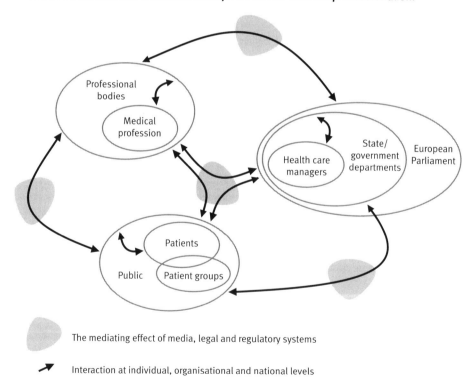

The mediating effect of media, legal and regulatory systems

Interaction at individual, organisational and national levels

and anecdote about modern medical practice, highlighting differences and similarities between the views of different stakeholders and shaping the nature of debate between them.

Ensuring effective action by the leaders of medical institutions

The medical profession should aim high. It should seek to define a modern professionalism that focuses on the interests and experiences of patients and requires doctors to take part in improving health services. It should create a clear framework for resolving the dilemmas facing today's doctors. This will require the leaders of the profession to help translate the new professional standards into everyday practice, bridging the gap between society's expectations and the day-to-day behaviour of doctors.

However, one obstacle here is the multiplicity of institutions that govern and represent the profession. There is no single 'lead' organisation that has a developmental role and also commands the respect of all doctors. That said, the Royal Colleges do have a responsibility for setting and implementing standards for different specialities, and the GMC has educational and regulatory roles through which the values of medical professionalism might be disseminated.

This process has already started and below we describe a range of recent initiatives. However, as a participant in a King's Fund seminar remarked, a 'visceral conversion' among doctors will be needed to ensure that patient interests become the drivers of medical professionalism (D Hutton, personal communication 2004). Current developments are significant and are certainly more than mere tokenism, but there is still scope for patient views and preferences to shape professional judgements more effectively. This will require a focus on professionalism at every stage of a medical career: in the curriculum of medical schools, in postgraduate education, in continuing professional development and in clinical governance arrangements.

It will also require leadership by example in the implementation of appraisal and revalidation. There is a danger that these procedures could become administrative exercises rather than a regular opportunity to review and reflect upon how far each doctor's clinical practice measures up to the standards of good medical practice. This issue is explored further in Case study 4: Reforming accountability (*see* pp 42–46).

Informing stakeholders about the new professionalism

Clear communication about what can be expected of doctors and what the standards for professional practice are will help to strengthen public trust. Once again, this task can be undertaken at a local or national level, between individual doctors and local groups of patients, or between medical institutions and the wider public. Case study 3: Clinical judgement and individual entitlement to care (*see* pp 37–42) looks at how honest communication about the reasons for clinical decisions and the constraints on medical practice can form part of high-quality clinical consultations and strengthen patients' trust in doctors.

Two other case studies on the issues of out-of-hours care and the organisation of hospital services show how service developments that will have profound effects on the experiences of patients have been made with little or no consultation with those patients. We argue that some form of input from patients is essential if their interests really are to shape changes in professional practice. This input can be secured in a variety of ways: for example, through local consultation exercises, patient involvement in policy-making or continuing dialogue between the medical profession and patient groups. We describe below some emerging arrangements for involving patients.

We have also made the case for more constructive engagement between the medical profession and the Government. Here there is a role for the media in highlighting complexity and encouraging debate. The current media focus on scandal and failure too often triggers defensive responses, with knock-on effects on public perceptions of the medical profession. Whether working alongside patients (as in current Department of Health policy collaboratives) or representing them in discussions with government, the profession must ensure that the impact of emerging policy on all aspects of patient interests is clearly explained. This will require new alliances between patients and doctors, based on an unswerving commitment by doctors to put patient interests at the heart of their professional judgements.

Raising public confidence in high-trust accountability arrangements for doctors

We suggest that the developments described above will rebuild trust in doctors. They will enable a reflective and responsive medical profession to review its practice, assess itself against stakeholder expectations and translate agreed standards for professional practice into everyday behaviour. With such systems in place, we believe there would be sufficient confidence in the medical profession to support a high-trust accountability system. Such a system could command public support while avoiding the risk of undermining professional motivation, standing and judgements.

Dilemmas in professional practice

Reference points to guide debate

In developing the following case studies, we have paid attention to three reference points that we believe should guide ongoing debate on medical professionalism:

- **All further debate must be undertaken with reference to improving patients' experiences of health care** Widely publicised examples of disastrous patient experiences have eroded patient confidence in medical regulation and undermined the compact between doctor, patient and state. Rebuilding public trust in medical professionalism and in open systems for its regulation will require an explicit commitment to shape professional duties around improving patients' experience of health care.

- **Individual doctors are always part of larger health systems** Given that patients' experiences are increasingly determined by the actions of a local set of health care workers and organisations within which doctors work, a wholly individual view of professionalism is inadequate. It is the actions of the health system 'in the round' that determine the overall quality of health care for individuals, and it is there where the tensions between the needs of individual patient and those of the general population emerge. Modern professionalism's commitment to work for the best interests of public and patients (in aggregate as well as individually) means sharing responsibility for the system as a whole and helping to seek out ways to improve it.

- **Reacting to the worst undermines the good** A dynamic and continuing process for reviewing professional identity and consequent responsibilities is needed. Such a process should not be seen solely as a reaction to past failures, as this would distract attention from the need constantly to reflect upon and improve standards and styles of practice. Regulatory and accountability mechanisms should avoid focusing solely on extreme cases, since this may encourage the misguided belief that professional identity should be based on the task of eliminating any possibility of bad practice. It should instead be a process that builds trust (including proportionate accountability) in a positive affirmation of professionalism for our time. Professionalism and regulation should aim to improve patients' experiences in a way that builds an ethos of continuing quality review and improvement.

Case study 1: Working patterns

As we have seen, the working patterns of doctors are changing. The reasons include:
- European legislation that restricts working hours
- more multi-disciplinary teamwork
- tighter managerial control over medical work
- expectations of improved work–life balance.

Here we use the example of the new arrangements for general practice out-of-hours (OOH) cover to examine how these changes affect traditional notions of professionalism.

Continuity, quality and out-of-hours primary care

The new General Medical Services (GMS) contract allows GPs to opt out of providing emergency care outside normal (8am–6.30pm) practice hours. Many GPs had already reduced their night-time workload by forming out-of-hours (OOH) co-operatives, in which large groups of GPs cover each other's surgeries – effectively delegating responsibility for OOH patient care to other local GPs. Each participating GP has thus been able to work fewer OOH shifts (perhaps four to six per quarter) than previously, when each practice provided its own OOH cover and working one night in three was common. Up to 90 per cent of GPs are expected to pull out of providing OOH cover.

Primary care trusts (PCTs) will take over the provision of OOH services from the end of 2004. There is no blueprint for these services to guide PCTs, but a range of solutions is emerging. These include: initial triage of all calls by NHS Direct nurses; the expansion of primary care services within hospital A&E departments; the introduction of nurses into OOH co-op rotas to make up for doctor shortfalls; and buying in OOH medical cover from private providers (such as deputising services – employing doctors who are not necessarily local GPs to provide OOH care).

Patient demand for out-of-hours care is growing, although the proportion of service users with serious medical problems requiring urgent hospitalisation remains small. Attempts to manage demand by educating patients about the appropriate indications for using emergency services have had little impact. Many patients are already used to receiving emergency care from an unknown GP. But under the new arrangements they may be directed towards any of the various services listed above. Information for patients about new OOH care is patchy and many will not understand the range of services now available. Moreover, there is little research evidence about how these changes might affect the overall quality of care that patients receive.

Patient groups were not formally involved in the GMS contract negotiations that resulted in these changes. A recent YouGov poll for the BBC (YouGov Ltd 2004) reported that about one-third of respondents were unhappy with the current arrangements, although almost 60 per cent felt that GPs should not have to work at night.

How do these new arrangements relate to the principles of modern professionalism?

The withdrawal of most GPs from OOH cover indicates a change in the way they are showing their commitment to service – traditionally demonstrated through a 24-hour duty of care. Modern professionalism is not necessarily manifested through an individual and continuous relationship between one doctor and one patient.

OOH co-operatives were an acknowledgement by GPs that the professional duty to meet every patient's needs was becoming harder to fulfil. They provided a way of sharing the responsibility for OOH care among a network of known peers, while retaining some input into standards and clinical governance. Withdrawal from OOH cover will remove most GPs from any involvement in setting or monitoring standards for new OOH providers.

For patients, the gradual evolution of OOH arrangements has obliged them to obtain emergency care first from doctors they were unlikely to know and now from a network of new providers about which they know little. A major professional challenge for GPs is to ensure that the new OOH arrangements to which they are directing their registered patients are of a sufficiently high standard to warrant handing over clinical responsibility each night. And a major test of their professionalism in the future may be their willingness to resume 24-hour responsibility if they have concerns about the quality of the new services.

In an environment that emphasises consumerism, choice and access, placing unbounded responsibility for 24-hour care on doctors may be counter-productive. One of the most significant findings of the Bristol Inquiry was that an heroic attempt to meet the demand for health care, without stopping to consider safety, quality or the need to manage demand, ran the risk of introducing a 'make do' culture that could become unsafe for patients and cause burn-out among professionals.

However, a reduction in a GP's personal responsibility for patients does not mean that altruism and a commitment to service are no longer important. It means that the professional obligation on doctors to do the best for patients is being discharged through new ways of working: for example, encouraging effective teamwork, building safety into complex systems and managing and improving health care services 'in the round'.

How can modern professionalism inform the future development of out-of-hours care?

Could the evolution of OOH policy have been usefully informed by the concept of modern medical professionalism? And can the concept still exert a useful influence on its implementation?

Modern medical professionalism, we have argued, requires a new compact that engages the public and other stakeholders more directly in negotiating the roles and responsibilities of all parties – particularly doctors. But patient groups and the general public were not directly involved in the development of OOH policy.

The views of the public could have been canvassed and used as evidence when considering different policy options. Around one-third of patients still want to see their usual doctor at night, while two-thirds accept the new limits to GP working hours. Does this constitute a public endorsement of the OOH arrangements in the new GMS contract? How should the expectations of a large minority of patients be balanced against those of the majority? Modern professionalism would require an explicit acknowledgement of the trade-off between the desire of some patients for 24-hour access to their doctor and the desire of some doctors for a better work–life balance.

Ongoing discussions with patient groups about refining OOH arrangements will need to take account of patient preferences and patient concerns. They will also have to acknowledge the difficulty of meeting the rising public demand for OOH care and the need to ensure that public expectations are manageable.

The increasing dependence on medical groups and multi-disciplinary teams creates new expectations of how doctors will maintain the quality of care. For modern medical professionals, collective approaches to monitoring care and maintaining standards will be just as important as individual efforts to maintain skills. Yet here too there will be new challenges, as services will be provided by doctors, nurses and in some cases other clinicians. Improvements in health care will need to be carried out in partnership with different professional groups, requiring new ways of working together. Whatever new challenges present themselves, disengagement and a willingness to let the PCT take on the responsibility are not options. Active participation in developing new and better services must become the norm.

Just as importantly, service providers should be willing to acknowledge problems and allocate the resources needed to solve them. If problems arise with OOH services, modern professionalism requires PCTs to engage with doctors as much as it requires doctors to address the problems themselves. As the second case study below also shows, maintaining quality may be as much about the organisation of care as about the skills and competence of individual clinicians. The duty to engage in improvement that we are advocating for doctors must be accompanied by a similar commitment by the provider to create the circumstances in which professionalism can flourish.

Case study 2: The organisation of medical work

The organisation of hospital services is changing. Innovations such as diagnostic and treatment centres, one-stop clinics and day-case surgery all illustrate the extent to which doctors are adapting to new ways of working.

Clinical judgement and organisational priorities – managing waiting lists

Reducing waiting times and waiting lists is a central aim of current health care policy. Recent initiatives include:

- enabling patients in selected specialities who have waited for longer than six months to choose to go to a different hospital
- centralised booking systems and pooled waiting lists for operations
- revising the balance between new patients, follow-up patients and urgent patients in outpatient clinics.

According to recent evidence submitted to the Health Select Committee, a number of patients at the Bristol Eye Hospital may have had poorer outcomes or even lost their sight as a result of such changes in hospital outpatient clinics (Harrad 2004). Follow-up outpatient appointments to monitor patients with long-term eye conditions and to assess their need for further treatment were not available because a high proportion of clinic appointments had been allocated to new patients. To reduce waiting times for first appointments, the booking systems had been set to include a large number of new patients in each clinic, but this created a shortage of follow-up appointments for patients with established disease who required regular monitoring.

One solution to this problem might be to regard high-risk patients as 'extras', and to appeal explicitly to the medical profession's sense of altruism and service to ensure that they are treated. To what extent are doctors still willing to put in this extra effort? And where they are willing, are hospital managers able to provide the necessary support (for example, overtime pay for clinic nurses)?

A second example of how managers and doctors may have differing views about how best to meet the needs of patients can be seen in the use of 'urgent' slots in outpatient clinics. The allocation of one or two slots for urgent referrals allows GPs to refer patients with severe problems to be seen by a consultant at short notice. To some managers, these empty slots (if they are not used) may seem inefficient, given the general concern about waiting times. Alternative approaches include establishing a dedicated emergency clinic (if staff and patient numbers permit) or assessing urgent patients in A&E. The doctors who advocate retaining these emergency slots see them as helping to create a flexible service that can respond quickly to GP and patient needs without dependence on casualty services. They offer rapid access to specialist opinion, allowing those patients requiring urgent intervention to be distinguished from those for whom telephone advice from the GP, or an early (but not urgent) appointment, will be enough.

What are the implications of changes to the organisation of medical work for modern professionalism?

How should modern medical professionals react to such changes? The clinical consequences of delayed follow-up can be devastating for some patients, yet current systems are removing control over this area of decision-making from doctors. This restricts the ethical duty of doctors to do what they perceive is needed to obtain the best possible clinical outcomes for their patients. It also restricts their freedom as professionals to control the content and organisation of their work.

But what of the other stakeholders? Government policy on waiting times and the systems introduced by medical managers are clearly responses to another dimension of patient interests: the public demand for faster access to health care. Surveys do reveal public dissatisfaction with long waits for NHS treatment, but at the individual level, it is surely also in the patient's interest to receive the best possible clinical outcome. A focus on one aspect of patient interest may be at the expense of other and equally important aspects, as the case of the Bristol Eye Hospital illustrates.

Media coverage is also important. Articles about long waiting lists and A&E waiting times have had a significant influence on government priorities. But there has been less coverage of the clinical consequences of reorganising services: media accounts of clinical failures have drawn more attention to the inadequate regulation of the doctor concerned than to any shortcomings in the organisation providing care. There is little debate about the pros and cons of different proposals for improving services and responding to public demand. And there is an opportunity for people in a position of medical leadership to broaden the debate.

How can modern professionalism inform future changes to the organisation of medical work?
Earlier we emphasised the importance of doctors engaging with the wider health service in order to improve services. But structural changes in the NHS have significantly reduced the involvement of doctors in hospital management roles that would, for example, enable them to help devise waiting list initiatives. A new compact might explicitly require doctors to help their organisation achieve its goals, but it should also include a reciprocal obligation on the part of organisations to involve doctors more directly in the management of health services (Edwards, Marshall, *et al* 2003).

There is a central role for medical institutions in this debate. How should they respond to the pressure on doctors to absorb more work in their clinics if patients need to be seen? Many doctors have long undertaken such additional work. But the new consultant contract has changed the climate for professional work in hospitals.

For consultants, a requirement to produce detailed work plans has replaced less clearly quantified employment arrangements. Greater accountability for the number of hours worked, the duration of clinics and the number of patients per clinic will provoke different responses from different doctors. Some will carry out their professional duties within the administrative boundaries set by the new contract, while others will take a different view of their commitment to patients and continue to extend clinics and see extra patients. What are the limits to professional obligation in this area?

Most importantly, wider public debate is needed about how to reconcile the competing interests of patients. The implicit decisions that used to be made to give one patient priority over another were often made without any effort to improve the service as a whole. But these decisions are increasingly open to public scrutiny, thanks to media accounts of delayed diagnosis and treatment. How can policies on clinic structure, waiting times and clinical priorities be better informed by public preferences without restricting doctors in their clinical judgement?

Case study 3: Clinical judgement and individual entitlement to care

One way in which doctors can improve the experience of patients is to be responsive to their preferences. But what happens when a patient's preference is for a course of action that a doctor does not think is clinically necessary?

Primary care management of headache

GPs often see patients who have been suffering from headaches for many months. A detailed clinical history (including psycho-social information) and physical examination can be used to distinguish headaches that have no serious underlying cause from those that do. The most common causes of headache are infection, depression, female hormone imbalance and drug side-effects. Brain tumours account for only 0.1 per cent of all headaches (Goadsby 2004), but anxiety about the possibility of a tumour or another serious cause for the headaches can be severe in some patients.

Many patients will be satisfied with their GP's opinion that, on the basis of their history and an examination, there is no serious underlying cause for the headache, which should therefore respond to pain control medicines. Some patients, however, may request a scan for reassurance. Research has shown that the 'yield' (positive finding) from MRI or CT scans is less than one per cent for people with migraine-type headaches and about two per cent for those with non-migraine headaches and a normal physical examination.

How should GPs reconcile their own clinical judgement with the preferences of patients? Open discussion about why the patient is worried, what the examination has shown and which treatments are available may help to build trust and allay anxiety. The consultation may end with GP and patient agreeing to monitor how symptoms change in response to treatment and to review the need for a scan at a later date. But in some cases, only referral for a scan will satisfy the patient.

Since MRI scans have no dangerous side effects, why should doctors bother trying to persuade a patient they do not need one? Some will do so because they have confidence in their clinical judgement and think a scan is clinically unnecessary. Others will see MRI scans as a scarce resource for which other patients with more worrying symptoms may have a more urgent need. They may refer the most anxious of patients, but only after discussing other options.

However, if the patient requesting a scan has private insurance, would the doctor who is concerned about scarcity refer them more readily? And what would happen if the investigation requested by the patient has harmful side effects? CT scans, for example, although not really harmful, do expose patients to high doses of radiation. Patients are free to make decisions about the risks and benefits associated with their preferences, and may well feel that the 'risks' associated with a CT scan are fully justified. But conditions other than headache may require investigations involving more significant risks: for example, the dye used in some scans can cause fatal allergic reactions in some people. If the risk of allergic reaction is the same as, or greater than, the likelihood of finding an abnormality on the scan, how should doctors react to the patient's preference? Should they respect the patient's right to take such risks or should they consider they have a professional duty to avoid harm?

How does the example of the primary care management of headache illustrate the challenges facing modern professionalism?
This case study describes the new relationship between doctors and patients and underlines the potential conflict between the rights of the individual and the rights of the general population to scarce health care resources. One line of argument would be that, because of their clinical experience and technical skill, doctors are best placed to judge what further benefits may accrue to a patient after a thorough examination. The likelihood of a serious underlying cause is low and this patient is less likely to benefit from referral to a specialist than other patients in future.

From an informed patient's perspective, however, the possibility of missing a serious diagnosis, however unlikely, may be unacceptable, given the awareness that a simple scan is available. In the past, such situations might have produced a clipped statement from the GP to the effect that no further investigation was necessary, and the patient would have been left with no opportunity to respond. Would an agreement by the GP to refer the patient for a scan, after open discussion about other options, exemplify what modern professionalism expects from an encounter between informed patient and respectful doctor?

This case study also highlights the pressure on GPs to manage demand – to balance the needs of current and future patients (what if the next patient through the door has a much greater need?) and to make referrals in accordance with evidence-based guidelines. The medical professionalism seminars run by the King's Fund revealed interesting differences of opinion among doctors and among other participants. Some argued that doctors were duty bound to do only what is best for the patient in front of them, with no regard for the needs of the wider population, while others said that it was defensible to make clinical decisions that took into account overall population needs. Interestingly, the international Medical Professionalism Project has explicitly incorporated the duty of social justice into its professional charter (Medical Professionalism Project 2002).

The growing prominence given to consumer 'rights' raises further issues for modern professionalism. Some may argue that the existence of private insurance cover is irrelevant to the decision about specialist referral, which should be made on purely clinical grounds. Others would acknowledge that people have a right to buy additional care. Individual decisions about referral are often made with reference to the needs of the wider population, with a 'referral threshold' determined by severity and the likelihood of identifying a treatable problem. Private insurance can be used to lower this threshold, granting access to care according to ability to pay. Doctors are regularly faced with such dilemmas – how to reconcile probability with their personal judgement – and are developing consultation styles to accommodate the discussions required. But the wider profession also has a role to play in highlighting examples of inequity and scarcity of services, as well as in shaping public opinion about the evidence base for clinical decisions (and in some cases the risks associated with further intervention).

How can modern professionalism inform our response to the issue of individual entitlement to care?

Scarcity affects every health service, and we believe that professional values must take account of this. Doctors should demonstrate altruism just as much in their relationship with the wider community of patients as with individual patients. We support the incorporation of the principle of social justice into the professional charter of the Medical Professionalism Project. However, the broad aims of improving patients' experiences, strengthening trust and responding to new expectations require professionals to respond to each patient individually. If discussion about the likely benefits of onward referral cannot allay anxiety, there is a strong case to be made for referral, irrespective of local guidelines.

This type of situation has been explored by the US managed care provider Harvard Pilgrim in association with the American College of Physicians and patient groups (Povar, Pomen *et al* 2004). Their work emphasises that the primary duty of doctors is to act for their patients, but that they have an additional duty to practice effectively and cost-efficiently. The researchers argue for the importance of preserving trust in the patient–clinician relationship while at the same time balancing the needs of the individual with those of the wider population. They suggest that doctor, patient and health plan (playing the same role as a primary care trust) all have a responsibility to exercise appropriate stewardship of health care resources, and that the processes of resource allocation should be open to public participation. Finally, they stress the obligation upon health plans to create an ethical environment for the delivery of care and to be open about any constraints upon the care that they can provide.

These US findings mirror our own discussion about the nature of modern professionalism. They emphasise the shared responsibility of doctors, patients and health care providers to place patient interest at the centre of decisions about health care – but not to the exclusion of all other factors. Their stress upon the obligation of health care providers as well as doctors to be open about the limits to available services is particularly important for the professional integrity of individual doctors.

Case study 4: Reforming accountability

Accountability is a central concept in any definition of modern professionalism. A more open system of accountability could connect professional values and behaviour with current social mores. An effective system can make it possible to identify problematic performance before it turns into error or causes avoidable harm. Indeed, such a system could offer many doctors better opportunities for improvement.

But an ineffectual system for ensuring accountability could undermine trust. There are two difficulties. Firstly, the system may become so bureaucratic, time-consuming and expensive that doctors may themselves lose trust in it and fail to participate in a meaningful way. Indeed, all the stakeholders who need to take part will require assurance that it is proportionate and realistic. Secondly, if there is an undue focus on the extreme scenarios of malicious behaviour, this could distort a system that has the potential to help bring about valuable improvements. It could even result in an exaggerated public perception of the risk of malicious intent, thus eroding trust, professional standing and motivation even further.

In practice, a variety of approaches to accountability are being used or developed. These include tightly defined performance indicators that address outcomes, qualitative assessments that take a more holistic view and managerial requirements that specify activity, workload and job planning. An effective system of accountability may need to combine approaches in order to address not only the domain of personal competence (such as behaviour, knowledge, skills and outcome) but also the doctor's contribution to the performance of the wider health system.

The consultant contract and appraisal-based arrangements for revalidation

The former consultant contract stipulated a specified number of sessions, with no formal monitoring of the consultant's workload. Consultants enjoyed considerable autonomy in organising their work and prioritising patients for outpatient clinics and operating sessions.

The new consultant contract creates a more explicit link between pay and volume of work and introduces managerial accountability through job plans. Furthermore, innovations, such as centralised booking systems, centralised administrative support and formal rules linking patient priority to waiting times, have reduced consultant control over which patients are seen when.

Current proposals for appraisal-based revalidation also aim to improve the accountability of medical practice. From 2005, doctors will be required to demonstrate to the GMC their continuing fitness to practise – in return, they will be given revalidation and a licence to practise.

The majority of doctors, it is now envisaged, will achieve this revalidation through participating in routine appraisal. In the words of the GMC's own guidance on revalidation: 'We believe that full participation in annual appraisal, with completed supporting documentation during the revalidation cycle, is a powerful indicator of a doctor's current fitness to practise.' The GMC goes on to advise doctors that 'if you use the appraisal route to revalidation, we will not normally want to see all the information you collect and keep to support your annual appraisals' (General Medical Council 2003).

To what extent do the new contract and the appraisal-based arrangements for revalidation meet modern professionalism's need for greater accountability? Or might they alienate doctors and undermine other, positive aspects of professional practice? How might doctors react to these changes in the core characteristics of their profession?

How do these new arrangements for reforming accountability demonstrate the principles of modern professionalism?
Revalidation is a good example of how professionalism is being reshaped in response to the multiple challenges described earlier. This new approach represents a dramatic shift in how the profession perceives self-regulation. Previously, this had been seen as individuals examining their consciences in relation to their own practice and trying to ensure that they met professional standards – the 'self' in self-regulation referred only to the individual. Now the profession as a whole is responsible for ensuring the accountability of individual doctors – the 'self' has been reinterpreted as the profession acting collectively to assure the quality of all doctors.

However, the forces that led to this change of approach by the medical profession also affected the state. If the profession was to keep the remaining freedoms and rewards of professional practice, it needed to show that it was worthy of public trust. But the Government also needed to respond to events, demonstrating its ability to represent the public interest and its desire to win public trust and greater control over the organisation of health care. So, in a similar move, the state also sought to change the self-regulation of individual doctors by introducing first appraisal and then the new contract, with its increased job planning and managerial control over the content of medical work.

The introduction of two new systems raised the possibility that efforts might be duplicated, so the proposal for revalidation came to be based on appraisal. But how do these initiatives by state and profession interact and what impact are they having on the conscience of the profession? By which we mean the understanding that individual doctors have of their own professional identity – an important factor in how doctors engage with the delivery of health care and its reform.

How can modern professionalism inform the issue of reforming accountability?

Modern professionalism emphasises that health care is a collaborative activity in which professionals share the responsibilities. So too with accountability: an effective system of ensuring fitness to practise has to be understood (risks and all) not only by doctors, managers and health care organisations, but crucially by public and patients. Accountability must build trust, meet current expectations and reinforce professional identity. An effective system needs to strike an agreed balance between rigour of oversight and continued clinical freedoms.

Medical organisations may need to involve the wider public in a discussion on how to introduce a more open and accountable approach to medical work – an approach that avoids regulatory systems that are too ambitious or too obtrusive. Peer review and appraisal may be sufficient to assess both the professional behaviour of doctors and their contribution to the health system. But they may not be suitable for demonstrating a doctor's continuing technical skill and knowledge. Here, accountability may require robust and comparable evidence of clinical performance accessible to professionals and non-professionals alike.

Leaders of the profession need to be aware of the effect that the new contract and appraisal-based validation may have on how doctors perceive modern professional practice. An increasingly complex system for ensuring accountability can undermine the professionalism it is supposed to safeguard. And doctors may feel less inclined to behave altruistically if they are excessively scrutinised. Here too, the profession may need to open a debate about the combined impact of these changes (actual and proposed). This must be done without running the risk of undermining professional motivation, morale and practice.

Taking modern professionalism forward

Establishing a new professional identity

This paper has looked at some of the issues that must be debated if we are to redefine professionalism for the 21st century and renew public trust in doctors. We turn now to the question of how we can put into practice a modern professionalism that centres on patient interest and strengthens the alliance between doctors and patients to guide the further development of health services.

We have described some of the dilemmas of modern medical practice, and have suggested areas where further debate is required to reconcile the interests of different groups. We believe that such debates would bring to doctors a renewed self-confidence about their individual and collective identity, upon which modern professionalism could be built.

This new identity would have to retain a view of professionals as highly skilled people possessing highly specialised – albeit more accessible – knowledge, observing rigorous ethical standards and having a sense of calling. But in order to respond to current social, economic and political trends, the new style of medical professional will also have to:

■ demonstrate a willingness to share decision-making with patients, should they so wish
■ reconcile the immediate clinical needs of the individual with the longer-term needs of the wider population
■ accept the need for accountability, to reassure patients and justify continued professional freedoms
■ participate in some form of performance review that reports on the content and quality of work

- engage in strategic and operational management in order to improve the patient's experience of care
- be willing to work in multi-speciality clinical teams.

And for their part, professional institutions will need to:
- form alliances with patient groups – as credible campaigners and advocates for patient needs – in negotiations with government over the provision of health services
- seek a new balance between the pursuit of their members' interests and those of the general public that is in line with changing social and political expectations and centred on patient interests
- develop opportunities to debate tensions between the interests of patients, doctors and government in the pursuit of better health services
- secure new arrangements for medical involvement in hospital and health care management.

Practical action

Here we propose five approaches to developing a new sense of professionalism based upon a realignment of interests between patients, doctors and society. In practice, a number of innovative initiatives, of the kind we describe, are already underway. But there is still a long way to go before they become a routine part of medical professional work. We propose the following approaches:
- new partnerships
- new processes
- new expectations
- stronger institutional leadership
- new relationships between patient, doctor and state.

New partnerships

New partnerships are needed to increase patient involvement in the development of standards and policy by medical institutions to improve the design of services and to reshape the interaction between patients and doctors. Recent examples include:

- pilot programmes inviting patients to influence teaching in medical schools
- lay representative groups within the Royal Colleges
- opportunities for joint public–professional debate about important current issues.

New processes

New processes are required to translate the standards of modern professionalism into everyday practice. Standards identified through the new compact must be translated into meaningful guidance for doctors and embedded into their understanding of professionalism. Recent examples include:

- incorporating assessment of professionalism into undergraduate and higher professional exams
- adapting assessment systems to accommodate the values and expectations of different cultures
- incentive systems for desired behaviour such as appraisal and revalidation
- contractual requirements to conform to explicit professional standards (such as those currently set out in *Good Medical Practice*).

New expectations

Recent examples of efforts to manage patient and public demand for health care include:

- media campaigns to influence the use of emergency services

- discussions between medical institutions and patient groups on the implications of the growth in public expectations
- better sources of information for patients about specific illnesses to support self-management and patient involvement in shared clinical decisions.

Stronger institutional leadership

The Royal Colleges, the British Medical Association (BMA), the GMC, the Academy of Royal Colleges and Professional Associations should be more rigorous in their efforts to incorporate expected standards into everyday practice. They should also be more open about issues where public and professional interests conflict and should encourage open debate on how to find a solution. Recent examples include:

- initiatives to incorporate the standards of *Good Medical Practice* into everyday practice in all specialities
- educational institutions incorporating professionalism into the examined curriculum.

New relationships between state, patients, managers and doctors

These new relationships should be based on more open debate about conflicts of interest and the trade-offs that characterise much health care policy and practice. This will require:

- structural changes in the organisation of clinical management, with more medical representation on hospital boards, as well as better working relationships and more closely aligned objectives between clinical and non-clinical managers
- new alliances between the medical profession, patient groups and their representatives
- new approaches to policy-making – illustrated to some extent by the current Department of Health policy collaboratives – in which explicit debate between stakeholders can shape policy
- a role for the media in triggering and supporting such debates.

Conclusion

We have argued that the medical profession must continue to adapt to significant changes in the expectations of society and government. If this does not happen, the consequences could be a loss of public confidence in the profession as a whole – although not necessarily in individual doctors – and in its ability to maintain professional standards through self-regulation.

The profession has come a long way in terms of the practice of individual doctors and of collective efforts by medical institutions to work with patients and the public. However, there has not yet been a 'visceral' shift in the willingness of the profession to place the interests of patients at the centre of all their judgements, nor in the willingness of doctors to engage with wider organisational changes aimed at improving the patient experience.

We have acknowledged the legitimacy of patients' expectations: their interests should lie at the heart of modern professionalism. We have therefore called upon institutions such as the GMC, the Royal Colleges and the medical schools to lead the way in working with patients and ensuring that the highest standards of medical practice are evident in the everyday work of doctors. However, we have also pointed out the diverse range of interests pursued by other parties with a stake in medical care and health services – particularly government and medical managers. And we have emphasised the need for government policy to be implemented in ways that enable the highest standards of professional practice to flourish.

Whether one believes that the interests of individual patients should be the overriding concern of medical professionals, or that their interests should be more explicitly balanced against those of other stakeholders, we have argued that conflicts of interest are bound to arise. The challenge for modern professionalism is to understand how these conflicts of interest affect patients. Medical institutions need to work with patient groups to identify the best possible balance between interests of individuals, the general population, the profession, medical organisations and the politicians.

We have proposed a number of practical ways forward. The collective institutions of the medical profession must show a determination to introduce *Good Medical Practice* into every aspect of medical work. But because of the current lack of medical leaders who are widely accepted by doctors and able to represent the profession, this proposal is easier to make than to implement. The successful development of modern professionalism will require the professional institutions to work together, sending consistent messages to all doctors. From such efforts, widely respected and broadly representative leaders may emerge.

Appraisal and revalidation are an important starting point, providing a means of assessing the progress made by individual doctors. But we need to confront the fact that doctors are increasingly being expected to play multiple professional roles and pursue a diverse range of objectives.

Equally important will be new forms of engagement between professional institutions, patients, government and managers, and the relationship these groups develop with the media. These links should form the basis of a new compact for modern professionalism and support more explicit consideration of the various interests pursued by all parties. Again, there has been much progress recently, with radical alterations in the lay membership of the GMC and several Royal Colleges, and with some medical schools considering how to promote 'professionalism' and patient-centredness as basic elements of medical training. But as shown by our case studies, difficult dilemmas will continue to arise – for which the solution must be to secure the greatest benefit to patients.

Continuing dialogue and compromise will be required from everyone with an interest in the workings of the medical profession. Medical professionalism needs to become the touchstone for understanding and resolving the inevitable challenges arising from diverse and conflicting expectations. It offers the best hope of finding a way forward that can also promote a common understanding of the role of a modern doctor in improving health care. We offer this paper as a starting point for the dialogue on which such a crucial development must be based.

Appendix: List of seminar participants

King's Fund medical professionalism seminars, April and May 2004

Ms Janet Askham
Professor Richard Baker
Ms Frances Blunden
Dr Sheila Borkett Jones
Dr Ed Borman
Professor Sir Cyril Chantler
Ms Lorelei Cooke
Ms Jane Cooper
Dr Jocelyn Cornwell
Ms Hilary De Lyon
Dr Rafey A Faruqui
Professor Louise Fitzgerald
Ms Rosalind Foster
Ms Margaret Goose
Professor Janet Grant
Mr Ben Griffith
Mr Andreas Hasman
Professor Sean Hilton
Professor Charlotte Humphrey
Professor Gillian Hundt
Professor Pali Hungin
Professor Sir Donald Irvine
Mr James Johnson
Dr Deborah Kirklin
Ms Kay Mackintosh

Mr Nizam Mamode
Mr Philip Masterton-Smith
Mrs Patricia Moberly
Professor Fiona Moss
Dr Roger Neighbour
Dr Raj Patel
Professor Sir Denis Pereira Gray
Mr David Pink
Dr Rita Renner
Dr John Riorden
Ms Joyce Robins
Mr Hugh Rogers
Dr David Roy
Mr Nigel Saunders
Dr Peter Simpson
Mr Tom Smith
Professor Dame Lesley Southgate
Professor John Spencer
Dr David Steel
Ms June Taylor
Mr Roger Taylor
Dr Mike Toop
Ms Jackie Wickham
Ms Sally Williams

King's Fund, Leeds Castle medical professionalism seminar, March 2003

Sir Roger Bannister
Professor Sir Graeme Catto
Professor Sir Cyril Chantler
Professor Angela Coulter
Mr Steve Dewar
Dr Jennifer Dixon
Professor Chris Ham
Professor Stephen Harrison
Sir Graham Hart
Dr David Haslam

Professor Christopher Hood
Professor Gillian Hundt
Dame Deirdre Hutton CBE
Professor Sir Donald Irvine
Dr Bruce Keogh
Sir Alan Langlands
Ms Sue Leggate
Ms Clara MacKay
Ms Isabel Nisbet
Dr Rebecca Rosen

Bibliography

Burkitt Wright E, Holcombe C, Salmon P (2004). 'Doctors' communication of trust, care and respect in breast cancer: qualitative study'. *British Medical Journal*, vol 328, pp 864–7.

Carter H. 'Surgeon admits guilt for killing'. *The Guardian*, 18 June 2004.

Cruess R, Cruess S (2003). 'Contemporary characteristics of the medical profession and the obligations required to sustain professionalism' in *Professionalism and the Modern Consultant: Central consultants and specialist committee consultation document No 1*. London: British Medical Association.

Edwards N, Marshall M, McLellan A, Abasi K (2003). 'Doctors and Managers: A problem without a solution? No, a constructive dialogue is emerging'. *British Medical Journal*, vol 326, pp 609–10.

General Medical Council (2001). *Good Medical Practice*, 3rd ed. London: General Medical Council.

General Medical Council (2003). *A Licence to Practise and Revalidation*. London: General Medical Council.

Goadsby P (2004). 'To scan or not to scan?'. *British Medical Journal*, vol 329, pp 469–70.

Ham C and Alberti G (2002). 'The medical profession, the public, and the government'. *British Medical Journal*, vol 324, pp 838–42.

Harrad R (2004). Quoted giving evidence on behalf of the Bristol Eye Hospital to the Health Select Committee. Available at: http://news.bbc.co.uk/2/hi/uk_news/politics/3085105.stm

Harrison S (2003). 'Medical autonomy and managerial authority in the National Health Service'. Paper presented at the King's Fund, Leeds Castle medical professionalism seminar, Leeds Castle, Kent.

Irvine D (2003). 'Medical Professionalism: Decision time', Duncan Memorial Lecture. Available at: http://www.kingsfund.org.uk/pdf/duncanmemorial.pdf

Mayor S (2001). 'Mortality for paediatric cardiac surgery at Bristol was twice that at other centres'. *British Medical Journal*, vol 323, pp 125.

Povar GJ, Blumen H, Daniel J, Daub S, Evans L, Holm RP, Levkovich N, McCarter AO, Sabin J, Snyder L, Sulmasy D, Vaughan P, Wellikson LD, Campbell A – Medicine as a Profession Managed Care Ethics Working Group (2004). 'Ethics in Practice: Managed care and the changing health care environment: Medicine as a Profession Managed Care Ethics Working Group Statement', *Annals of Internal Medicine*, vol 141:2, pp 131–6.

Sox H (2002). 'Medical Professionalism Project: Medical professionalism in the new millennium – a physician's charter'. *Annals of Internal Medicine*, vol 136, pp 243–6.

Yougov Ltd (2004). *Exploring Attitudes to GPs*. Web report available at: http://www.yougov.com/yougov_website/asp_besPollArchives/pdf/ TEL040101014_1.pdf

Linked publications

We publish a range of resources on different aspects of health care, including reports, research papers and free summaries. See below for a selection. For our full range of current titles, visit www.kingsfund.org.uk/publications or call Sales and Information on 020 7307 2591.

London's Mental Health Workforce: A review of recent developments
Leena Genkeer, Pippa Gough and Belinda Finlayson

Across the NHS, recruiting and retaining staff is a major challenge. In mental health services, the workforce is getting older, violence and harassment can cause problems, and heavy workloads are common. This working paper, published as part of a wider King's Fund inquiry into London's mental health services, argues that measures are needed to improve the working environment for acute mental health nurses in particular, and that cross-agency working is crucial.

Apr 2003 58pp **Free**
Download at: www.kingsfund.org.uk/publications

Great to Be Grey: How can the NHS recruit and retain more older staff?
Sandra Meadows

Experienced and skilled older workers are leaving the NHS early in ever-increasing numbers, driven into early retirement by heavy workloads, long hours and low morale. This research paper looks at how early retirement affects the NHS and explores how other sectors recruit and retain older staff. It argues that sustained commitment from the Government and NHS management – backed up by new kinds of flexibility and a determination to put 'people issues' at the heart of performance management – will be crucial if older people are to be valued as key contributors to the NHS.

ISBN 1 85717 471 2 Dec 2002 44pp **£8.00**
Download summary at: www.kingsfund.org.uk/publications

Five-Year Health Check: A review of Government health policy 1997–2002
Anna Coote and John Appleby (eds)

When the Labour Government came to power in 1997, it promised to 'save the NHS' by cutting waiting lists, improving service quality, raising spending, and reducing health inequalities. Five years on, this report scrutinises progress against pledges made by the Government in areas such as funding, staffing and quality of care. It argues that money alone, while crucial, will not build a new NHS, and that professional, motivated staff and a focus on wider health issues also have a key role to play.

ISBN 1 85717 463 1 Apr 2002 138pp **£7.99**
Download the introduction at www.kingsfund.org.uk/free

Hidden Assets: Values and decision-making in the NHS
Bill New and Julia Neuberger

What do values really mean for a modern, publicly owned health service? On what basis can staff and policy-makers resolve the inherent tensions between equally valid – but competing – priorities, such as equity of access and increased patient choice, or efficiency and effectiveness? Based on a series of King's Fund seminars with distinguished thinkers and practitioners from UK health circles and beyond, this publication combines analysis and case studies to show how values can successfully translate into health care provision, and argues that for values to 'live' as an organisational reality, trade-offs must be visible, managed and explicit.

ISBN 1 85717 458 5 2002 230pp **£17.00**
Download a sample chapter at www.kingsfund.org.uk/free

Racism in Medicine: An agenda for change
Naaz Coker (ed)

Racism weakens the NHS and damages the health of the individuals who endure discrimination. Using historical perspectives, research and anecdotes from culturally diverse contributors, and highlighting examples of bad and good practice, this book contributes to reinforcing a growing determination in the NHS to eradicate racist practices. It argues that, unless the NHS can show that prejudice is unequivocally a thing of the past, it will fail to make use of the skills, talents and time of a significant number of its workforce.

ISBN 1 85717 407 0 Jun 2001 242pp **£15.99**

Ethics and Health Care
Julia Neuberger

Human research is a vital part of furthering knowledge but it also throws up a variety of ethical problems. This report examines the work of research ethics committees in the UK and compares practice with guidelines from the Department of Health and the Royal College of Physicians.

ISBN 1 87060 729 5 1992 48pp **£6.99**